DER BANNERTRÄGER

„Ob im Glück oder im Unglück, ob in der Freiheit oder im Gefängnis, ich bin meiner Fahne, die heute des Deutschen Reiches Staatsflagge ist, treu geblieben."

Adolf Hitler

In *The House that Hitler Built* (see Extract 35), S. H. Roberts says, in a footnote, "In Munich in the early Autumn of 1936 I saw coloured pictures of Hitler in the actual silver garments of the Knight of the Grail; but these were soon withdrawn. They gave the show away; they were too near the truth of Hitler's mentality."

HITLER and the Rise of the Nazis

D. M. PHILLIPS

Mein Kampf

Eine Abrechnung
von
Adolf Hitler

1. Band

1 9 2 5

Verlag Franz Eher Nachfolger G. m. b. H.
München NO 2

THE ARCHIVE SERIES Hill and Fell

THE ARCHIVE SERIES

General Editors: C. P. Hill and G. H. Fell

Hitler and the Rise of the Nazis

D. M. Phillips
Senior History Master, Trinity Grammar School, Melbourne

Edward Arnold (Publishers) Ltd. London

THE ARCHIVE SERIES

at present contains the following titles:

Disraeli and Conservatism *by* Robin Grinter.
Lenin and the Russian Revolutions *by* F. W. Stacey.
British Imperialism in the Late 19th Century *by* L. R. Gardiner and J. H. Davidson.
The Liberals and the Welfare State *by* R. D. H. Seaman.
Mussolini and the Fascist Era *by* Desmond Gregory.
Hitler and the Rise of the Nazis *by* D. M. Phillips.
The General Strike *by* C. L. Mowat.
Anglo–Russian Relations 1854–1939 *by* F. W. Stacey.
The Rise of the Labour Party in Great Britain *by* G. R. Smith.

Further titles are in preparation.

Printed in Great Britain by
Cox & Wyman Ltd., London, Reading and Fakenham

General Preface

The aim of the Archive Series is to provide historical source material suitable for use in secondary schools. Today it is widely and strongly felt to be right to introduce school students of history, in some elementary way, to the raw materials of the subject. The booklets in this series will provide selections of material on historical topics in a form suitable for students of fifteen to seventeen years of age. Each topic has been selected for its interest and importance. The material ranges widely: extracts from newspapers, letters, speeches, diaries, treaties, novels, statutes, and autobiographies are all represented.

Teachers, we imagine, will find the booklets useful in various ways: as a means to enrich a syllabus, as a supplement to textbooks, as the basis for elementary investigation of sources themselves, as illustrations of policies or attitudes, or merely as an occasional change from the normal routine. The series has a uniform format for ease of reference, but the author of each booklet has adopted his own plan of approach. We hope that the series will stimulate interest and increase understanding.

C. P. H.
G. H. F.

Acknowledgments

Detailed sources are given at the end of the book for each extract, but the publishers would also like to acknowledge permission to reprint copyright material from the following:

Heinz Guderian: Sir Basil Liddell Hart
Herman Rauschning: Dr. L. Mohrenwitz.

Endpapers: Ullstein Bilderdienst, Berlin (The Election Poster). The executors of David Low and the *Evening Standard* (the cartoons).

Cover: This shows the title page and the first text page from the first edition of *Mein Kampf.*

Contents

Introduction

This book attempts to give some understanding of one man and the party he led; it is not intended to be a short documentary history of Germany between 1918 and 1945.

The reader who is not well acquainted with Nazism may have difficulty in understanding its origins and growth. If he looks for the orderly development of government and parties he will remain confused. Politically, the German scene was tense and disturbed, extreme political groups predominated, detached judgment of the country's problems was often difficult or absent altogether, legislation for most of the thirties was by personal decree and the influence of one man was crucial. Germany's economy was at certain periods chaotic and no individual escaped unscathed. The defeat suffered in 1918 hurt deeply, German hopes for the future were uncertain, and, for a number of Germans, the resolving of their many problems lay in the hands of the extremists.

Rather more than half of the documents have been drawn from the period before Hitler gained power in 1933 in order to illuminate Nazi thinking and penetrate the personality and thoughts of Hitler—although it may be argued that these amount to much the same thing. Perhaps the clearest view of Nazism can be gained from studying Hitler's *Mein Kampf* and his many speeches and, accordingly, great use has been made of these sources. It is hoped that a picture both of the man and his movement will emerge from these documents.

1. Germany, 1918 - 1933

HITLER'S REACTION TO THE FIRST WORLD WAR

1. *Adolf Hitler was among the first to volunteer for army service in August 1914. He served throughout the war, and with bravery and distinction. He was awarded the Iron Cross, First Class, an unusual honour for a corporal. In November 1918 Hitler was in hospital recovering his sight after a British gas attack. An elderly pastor announced that Germany had lost the war:*

> With the next few days came the most astonishing information of my life. The rumours grew more and more persistent. I was told that what I had considered to be a local affair was in reality a general revolution. In addition to this, from the front came the shameful news that they wished to capitulate! What! Was such a thing possible? . . . I broke down completely when the old gentleman tried to resume his story by informing us that we must now end this long war, because the war was lost, he said, and we were at the mercy of the victor. . . . It was impossible for me to stay and listen any longer. Darkness surrounded me as I staggered and stumbled back to my ward and buried my aching head between the blankets and pillow.
>
> I had not cried since the day that I stood beside my mother's grave.

THE TREATY OF VERSAILLES

The Treaty of Versailles was signed on June 28th, 1919, and contained hundreds of articles concerning the League of Nations, boundaries and self-determination, German rights, disarmament, reparations and guarantees. The three extracts that follow are intended to show three only of the more important and contentious articles—the reduction of Germany's forces, the 'war guilt' clause and the reparations clause (the amount finally fixed being £stg. 6,600,000,000).

9

2. Article 160

By a date which must not be later than March 31st, 1920, the German Army must not comprise more than seven divisions of infantry and three divisions of cavalry.

After that date the total number of effectives in the Army of the States constituting Germany must not exceed one hundred thousand men, including officers and establishments of depots. The Army shall be devoted exclusively to the maintenance of order within the territory and to the control of the frontiers.

The total effective strength of officers, including the personnel of staff, whatever their composition, must not exceed four thousand.

3. Article 231

The Allied and Associated Governments affirm and Germany accepts the responsibility of Germany and her Allies for causing all the loss and damage to which the Allied and Associated Governments and their nationals have been subjected as a consequence of the war imposed upon them by the aggression of Germany and her Allies.

4. Article 232

The Allied and Associated Governments recognize that the resources of Germany are not adequate, after taking into account permanent diminutions of such resources which will result from other provisions of the present Treaty, to make complete reparation for all such loss and damage.

The Allied and Associated Governments, however, require, and Germany undertakes, that she will make compensation for all damage done to the civilian population of the Allied and Associated Powers and to their property during the period of the belligerency of each as an Allied or Associated Power against Germany by such aggression by land, by sea and from the air.

THE VIEWS OF HITLER AND OTHERS ON THE TREATY

5. *Two days after the signing of the Peace Treaty* The Times *special correspondent in Germany sounded this warning:*

If there is one country that the Germans are determined to get even with it is France.

The Germans will try by every means to foster differences between the Allies. To isolate France, to render the pledges of Great Britain and the United States null and void is the dominating idea of the individual German serving no impulse but his own; and one hears talk about a next war, first with Poland, later with France, when financial stability is restored and the treaty provisions are forgotten. . . . Never was it more necessary for the Allies to watch Germany closely.

6. *In* Mein Kampf *Hitler wrote of the stand he took against the treaty:*

. . . millions of Germans saw in the Treaty of Versailles a just castigation for the crime we had committed at Brest-Litowsk. Thus they considered all opposition to Versailles as unjust and in many cases there was an honest moral dislike of such a proceeding. And this was also the reason why the shameless and monstrous word 'Reparations' came into common use in Germany. This hypocritical falsehood appeared to millions of our exasperated fellow-countrymen as the fulfilment of a higher justice. It is a terrible thought, but the fact was so. The best proof of this was the propaganda which I initiated against Versailles by explaining the Treaty of Brest-Litowsk. I compared the two treaties with one another, point by point, and showed how in truth the one treaty was immensely humane, in contra distinction to the inhuman barbarity of the other. The effect was very striking. Then I spoke on this theme before an assembly of two thousand persons, during which I often saw three thousand six hundred hostile eyes fixed on me. And three hours later I had in front of me a swaying mass of righteous indignation and fury. A great lie had been uprooted from the hearts and brains of a crowd composed of thousands of individuals and a truth had been implanted in its place.

7. *He also saw the political advantages of doing so:*

As for myself, I then saw clearly that for the small group which first composed our movement the question of war guilt had to be cleared up, and cleared up in the light of historical truth. A preliminary condition for the future success of our movement was that it should bring knowledge of the meaning of the peace treaties to the minds of the popular masses. In the opinion of the masses, the peace treaties then signified a democratic success. Therefore, it was necessary to take the opposite side and dig ourselves into the minds of the people as the enemies of the peace treaties; so that later on, when the naked truth of this despicable swindle would be disclosed in all its hideousness, the people would recall the position which we then took and would give us their confidence.

HITLER'S VIEWS ON PARLIAMENTARY DEMOCRACY AND HIS ALTERNATIVE TO IT

8. *Also in* Mein Kampf *Hitler recalled that his opposition to parliamentary government stemmed from his experience of it as a young man in Vienna:*

Then I began to reflect seriously on the whole thing. I went to the Parliament whenever I had any time to spare and watched the spectacle silently but attentively. I listened to the debates, as far as they could be understood, and I studied the more or less intelligent features of those 'elect' representatives of the various nationalities which composed that motley State. Gradually I formed my own ideas about what I saw.

A year of such quiet observation was sufficient to transform or completely destroy my former convictions as to the character of this parliamentary institution. I no longer opposed merely the perverted form which the principle of parliamentary representation had assumed in Austria. No. It had become impossible for me to accept the system in itself. Up to that time I had believed that the disastrous deficiencies of the Austrian Parliament were due to the lack of a German majority, but now I recognized that the institution itself was wrong in its very essence and form.

9. *Hitler saw more dangerous features of democratic government:*

Democracy, as practised in Western Europe today, is the forerunner of Marxism. In fact the latter would not be conceivable without the former. Democracy is the breeding-ground in which the bacilli of the Marxist world pest can grow and spread. By the introduction of parliamentarianism democracy produced an abortion of filth and fire, the creative fire of which, however, seems to have died out.

10. *In* Mein Kampf *Hitler drew conclusions from his attacks on parliamentary democracy as these two extracts show:*

One truth which must always be borne in mind is that the majority can never replace the man. The majority represents not only ignorance but cowardice. And just as a hundred blockheads do not equal one man of wisdom, so a hundred poltroons are incapable of any political line of action that requires moral strength and fortitude.

11. *Where can we draw the line between public duty and personal honour?*

Must not every genuine leader renounce the idea of degrading himself to the level of a political jobber?

And, on the other hand, does not every jobber feel the itch to 'play politics', seeing that the final responsibility will never rest with him personally but with an anonymous mass which can never be called to account for their deeds?

Must not our parliamentary principle of government by numerical majority necessarily lead to the destruction of the principle of leadership?

Does anybody honestly believe that human progress originates in the composite brain of the majority and not in the brain of the individual personality?

Or may it be presumed that for the future human civilization will be able to dispense with this as a condition of its existence?

But may it not be that, today, more than ever before, the creative brain of the individual is indispensable?

The parliamentary principle of vesting legislative power in the decision of the majority rejects the authority of the individual and puts a numerical quota of anonymous heads in its place.

12. *In 1924 Hitler reflected on his youth in Vienna where he had formed views on the principle of political leadership:*

The problems to be dealt with are not put to the vote of the majority; but they are decided upon by the individual and as a guarantee of responsibility for those decisions he pledges all he has in the world and even his life.

The objection may be raised here, that under such conditions it would be very difficult to find a man who would be ready to devote himself to so fateful a task. The answer to that objection is as follows:

We thank God that the inner spirit of our German democracy will of itself prevent the chance careerist, who may be intellectually worthless and a moral twister, from coming by devious ways to a position in which he may govern his fellow-citizens. The fear of undertaking such far-reaching responsibilities, under German democracy, will scare off the ignorant and the feckless.

But should it happen that such a person might creep in surreptitiously it will be easy enough to identify him and apostrophize him ruthlessly, somewhat thus: 'Be off, you scoundrel. Don't soil these steps with your feet; because these are the steps that lead to the portals of the Pantheon of History, and they are not meant for place-hunters but for men of noble character.'

Such were the views I formed after two years of attendance at the sessions of the Viennese Parliament. Then I went there no more.

13. *Hitler stood trial in 1923 for his part in the Munich 'beer-hall putsch' and proclaimed to the court:*

The army we have formed is growing from day to day ... I nourish the proud hope that one day the hour will come when these rough companies will grow to battalions, the battalions to regiments, the regiments to divisions, that the old cockade will be taken from the mud, that the old flags will wave again, that there will be a reconciliation at the last great divine judgment which we are prepared to face... For it is not you, gentlemen, who pass judgment on us. That judgment is spoken by the eternal court of history. What judgment you will hand down, I know. But that court will not ask us: 'Did you commit high treason, or did you not?' That court will judge us, the Quartermaster-General of the old Army (Ludendorff), his officers and soldiers, as Germans who wanted only the good of their own people and the Fatherland; who wanted to fight and die. You may pronounce us guilty a thousand times over, but the goddess of the eternal court of history will smile and tear to tatters the brief of the State Prosecutor and the sentence of this court. For she acquits us.

QUESTIONS:
1. Briefly summarize the three Versailles Treaty articles.
2. What did Hitler consider was the German people's reaction to the treaty? What did he do to change this reaction?
3. Hitler was opposed to the principle of democratic parliamentary government. What did he see as its defects and what were the dangers it bred?
4. On what grounds did Hitler believe parliamentary democracy incapable of producing a leader?
5. Read Extracts 12 and 13. Do you regard them as mere expressions of defiance?

2. National Socialism, 1918 - 1933

EARLY DAYS OF THE NAZI PARTY

14. *In 1919 Hitler was invited to join the German Workers' Party which, as he wrote later, had 'nothing but obvious good faith and good intentions'. In its early years this forerunner of the Nazi Party was often short of funds, and lacked an organization for putting itself on a firm footing. Kurt Ludecke, who was one of the party's first members, recounted these days:*

The organization lived from day to day financially, with no treasury to draw on for lecture-hall rentals, printing costs, or the thousand-and-one expenses which threatened to swamp us. The only funds we could count on were membership dues, which were small, merely a drop in the bucket. Collections at mass meetings were sometimes large, but not to be relied on. Once in a while, a Nazi sympathizer would make a special contribution, and in a few cases these gifts were really substantial. But we never had money enough. Everything demanded outlays that were, compared to our exchequer, colossal. Many a time, posting the placards for some world-shaking meeting, we lacked money to pay for the paste.

15. *One of the most dramatic acts of the Nazis in the twenties was the attempt to seize power in Bavaria and establish a national government. The following speech by Hitler was made to a meeting organized by the Nazis in a Munich beer-hall:*

The Bavarian Ministry is removed. I propose that a Bavarian government shall be formed... The government of the November criminals and the Reich President are declared to be removed. A new National Government will be nominated this very day, here in Munich. A German National Army will be formed immediately. ... I propose that, until accounts have been finally settled with the November criminals, the direction of policy in the National Government be taken over by me... The task of the provisional German National Government is to organize the march on that sinful Babel, Berlin, and save the German people... Tomorrow will see either a National Government in Germany or us dead.

THE NAZI PARTY PROGRAMME

16. *Possibly the clearest statement of the National Socialist Party's objectives is to be found in the twenty-five point programme adopted in 1920 and reaffirmed six years later. The following are extracts from the programme:*

 1. We demand the union of all Germans to form a Great Germany on the basis of the right of the self-determination enjoyed by nations.
 2. We demand equality of rights for the German People in its dealings with other nations, and abolition of the Peace Treaties of Versailles and St. Germain.

3. We demand land and territory [colonies] for the nourishment of our people and for settling our superfluous population.

4. None but members of the nation may be citizens of the State.

8. All non-German immigration must be prevented.

10. It must be the first duty of each citizen of the State to work with his mind or with his body. The activities of the individual may not clash with the interests of the whole, but must proceed within the frame of the community and be for the general good.

18. We demand ruthless prosecution of those whose activities are injurious to the common interest.

22. We demand abolition of a paid army and formation of a national army.

23. We demand legal warfare against conscious political lying and its dissemination in the Press.

24. We demand liberty for all religious denominations in the State, so far as they are not a danger to it and do not militate against the moral feelings of the German race.

HITLER'S VIEW OF GERMAN NATIONALISM

17. *There was a strong nationalist basis to Nazi thought. In* Mein Kampf *Hitler looked back on the youthful nationalist stirrings within him and distinguished two forms of nationalism, the dynastic and racial:*

The youth were educated politically at a time when the citizens of a so-called national State for the most part knew little of their own nationality except the language. Of course, I did not belong to the hedgers. Within a little while I had become an ardent 'German National', which had a different meaning from the party significance attached to that phrase today.

I developed very rapidly in the nationalist direction, and by the time I was fifteen years old I had come to understand the distinction between dynastic patriotism and nationalism based on the concept of folk, or people, my inclination being entirely in favour of the latter.

18. *Following from this, Hitler and the Nazis emphasized the consolidation of 'pure' elements within the community* (Gemeinschaft). *The ideal was to be restated many times by the Nazis, and Hitler in 1939 expressed it clearly and simply:*

> A community . . . cannot primarily be created by the power of compulsion, but only by the compelling power of an idea, that is, by the strenuous exertions of constant education: National Socialism aims at the establishment of a real national community. . . . It is precisely the beauty of this ideal which compels man to go on working and consequently to strive after it undauntedly. This is the difference between the party programmes of a vanished past and the ultimate aim of National Socialism. They contained variously formulated conceptions or aims of an economic, political or denominational character. They were, however, only applicable to their own age, and consequently limited. National Socialism, on the other hand, has set itself an aim in its community of the nation which can only be attained and held by continuous and constant education.

19. *Closely related to the ideal of* Gemeinschaft *was the notion of Aryan superiority, reference to which is frequently made in* Mein Kampf:

> The adulteration of the blood and racial deterioration conditioned thereby are the only causes that account for the decline of ancient civilizations; for it is never by war that nations are ruined, but by the loss of their powers of resistance, which are exclusively a characteristic of pure racial blood. In this world everything that is not of sound stock is like chaff. Every historical event in the world is nothing more nor less than a manifestation of the instinct of racial self-preservation, whether for weal or woe.

20. The constructive powers of the Aryan and that peculiar ability he has for the building up of a culture are not grounded in his intellectual gifts alone. If that were so they might only be destructive and could never have the ability to organize. . . . And the world is indebted to the Aryan mind for having developed the concept of

'mankind'; for it is out of this spirit alone that the creative force has come which in a unique way combined robust muscular power with a first class intellect and thus created the monuments of human civilization.

HITLER, THE STATE AND THE INDIVIDUAL

21. *Nazi racial concepts and the idea of* Gemeinschaft *presented no conflict to the Nazis for rights would willingly be foregone by the individual for the sake of the whole community. Hitler often made this point and this extract is taken from* Mein Kampf:

A strong national Reich which recognizes and protects to the largest possible measure the rights of its citizens both within and outside its frontiers can allow freedom to reign at home without trembling for the safety of the State. On the other hand, a strong national Government can intervene to a considerable degree in the liberties of the individual subject as well as in the liberties of the constituent states without thereby weakening the ideal of the Reich; and it can do this while recognizing its responsibility for the ideal of the Reich, because in these particular acts and measures the individual citizen recognizes a means of promoting the prestige of the nation as a whole.

THE GERMANIC COMMUNITY AND LIVING SPACE

22. *The incorporation of all Germans into the Reich was a positive part of racial policy and was one of the earliest features in Hitler's political thinking. Hitler, himself an Austrian, wrote in* Mein Kampf:

German-Austria must be restored to the great German Motherland. And not indeed on any grounds of economic calculation whatsoever. No, no! Even if the union were a matter of economic indifference, and even if it were to be disadvantageous from the economic standpoint, still it ought to take place. People of the same blood should be in the same Reich. The German people will have no right to engage in a colonial policy until they shall have brought all their children together in the one State.

When the territory of the Reich embraces all the Germans and finds itself unable to assure them a livelihood, only then can the moral right arise, from the need of the people, to acquire foreign territory. The plough is then the sword; and the tears of war will produce the daily bread for the generations to come.

23. *The Aryan instinct for self-preservation involved the need for space in which to live* (Lebensraum)—*a need made all the more pressing by the terms of the Treaty of Versailles. Hitler wrote in 1924:*

One must calmly and squarely face the truth that it certainly cannot be part of the dispensation of Divine Providence to give a fifty times larger share of the soil of this world to one nation than to another. In considering this state of affairs today, one must not allow existing political frontiers to distract attention from what ought to exist on principles of strict justice. If this earth has sufficient room for all, then we ought to have that share of the soil which is absolutely necessary for our existence.

Of course people will not voluntarily make that accommodation. At this point the right of self-preservation comes into effect. And when attempts to settle the difficulty in an amicable way are rejected the clenched hand must take by force that which was refused to the open hand of friendship.

THE JEWS AND MARXISTS

24. *Beliefs in Aryan superiority, the German community and* Lebensraum *meant that the Nazis regarded other races as inferior. In* Mein Kampf *Hitler related how in pre-war Vienna he first realized the connection between them:*

I gradually discovered that the Social Democratic Press was predominantly controlled by Jews. But I did not attach special importance to this circumstance, for the same state of affairs existed also in other newspapers. But there was one striking fact in this connection. It was that there was not a single newspaper with which Jews were connected that could be spoken of as National, in the meaning that my education and convictions attached to that word.

Making an effort to overcome my natural reluctance, I tried to read articles of this nature published in the Marxist Press; but in doing so my aversion increased all the more. And then I set about learning something of the people who wrote and published this mischievous stuff. From the publisher downwards, all of them were Jews. I recalled to mind the names of the public leaders of Marxism, and then I realized that most of them belonged to the Chosen Race—the Social Democratic representatives in the Imperial Cabinet as well as the secretaries of the Trades Unions and the street agitators. Everywhere the same sinister picture presented itself. I shall never forget the row of names—Austerlitz, David, Adler, Ellenbogen and others. One fact became quite evident to me. It was this alien race that held in its hands the leadership of that Social Democratic Party with whose minor representatives I had been disputing for months past. I was happy at last to know for certain that the Jew is not a German.

25. *By 1924 Hitler had come to regard himself as a crusader against Jews and Marxists:*

. . . If the Marxist teaching were to be accepted as the foundation of the life of the universe, it would lead to the disappearance of all order that is conceivable to the human mind. And thus the adoption of such a law would provoke chaos in the structure of the greatest organism that we know, with the result that the inhabitants of this earthly planet would finally disappear.

Should the Jew, with the aid of his Marxist creed, triumph over the people of this world, his Crown will be the funeral wreath of mankind, and this planet will once again follow its orbit through ether, without any human life on its surface, as it did millions of years ago.

And so I believe today that my conduct is in accordance with will of the Almighty Creator. In standing guard against the Jew I am defending the handiwork of the Lord.

26. *It was a belief that remained with him. In a speech delivered in the Reichstag in 1939 he said:*

One thing I should like to say on this day which may be memorable for others as well as for us Germans: In the course of my life I have very often been a prophet, and have usually been ridiculed for it. During the time of my struggle for power, it was in the first instance the Jewish race which only received my prophecies with laughter when I said that I would one day take over the leadership of the State, and with it that of the whole nation, and that I would then among many other things settle the Jewish problem. Their laughter was uproarious, but I think that for some time now they have been laughing on the other side of their face. Today I will once more be a prophet: If the international Jewish financiers in and outside Europe should succeed in plunging the nations once more into a world war, then the result will not be the bolshevization of the earth, and thus the victory of Jewry, but the annihilation of the Jewish race in Europe!

HITLER AND THE NECESSITY FOR STRUGGLE

27. *Another consistent theme in Nazi thinking was the belief that struggle was an essential part of the movement. In 1933 Hitler spoke of the Nazi fight against Communism as being part of Germany's destiny:*

If a single people in Western or Central Europe were to succumb to Bolshevism, this poison would spread farther and would destroy that which is today the oldest and fairest cultural treasure in the world. By taking upon herself this struggle against Bolshevism Germany is but fulfilling, as so often before in her history, a European mission.

28. *He was well aware that right by itself was not sufficient. He wrote in 1924:*

If Social Democracy should be opposed by a more truthful teaching, then, even though the struggle be of the bitterest kind, this truthful teaching will finally prevail, provided it be enforced with equal ruthlessness.

29. *His contempt for inaction is evident in this extract from* Mein Kampf:

If in the past our ancestors had based their political decisions on similar pacifist nonsense as our present generation does, we should not possess more than one-third of the national territory that we possess today and probably there would be no German nation to worry about its future in Europe.

30. *Hitler felt that struggle demanded almost superhuman qualities and in this regard he was conscious of his own rôle. Two months after the start of the Second World War he spoke of the epic proportions that the war would assume:*

If we come through this struggle victoriously—and we shall—our time will enter into the history of our people. I shall stand or fall in this struggle. I shall never survive the defeat of my people. No capitulation to the forces outside; no revolution from within.

NAZISM AND INTELLECTUAL ACHIEVEMENT

31. *On a number of occasions Hitler showed that the man of scholarship and intellectual attainment had little to offer alongside the man of strong will and feeling (see also Extracts 20 and 38). In 1924 he wrote:*

The knights of the pen and the literary snobs of today should be made to realize that the great transformations which have taken place in this world were never conducted by a goosequill. No. The task of the pen must always be that of presenting the theoretical concepts which motivate such changes. The force which has ever and always set in motion great historical avalanches of religious and political movements is the magic power of the spoken word. . . .
He who is not capable of passionate feeling and speech was never chosen by Providence to be the herald of its will. Therefore a writer should stick to his ink-bottle and busy himself with theoretical questions, if he has the requisite ability and knowledge. He has not been born or chosen to be a leader.

32. *The arts and sciences took an increasingly nationalist and racial aspect after 1933. Much of what took place was foreshadowed by Hitler in 1924:*

> In order to form a correct judgment of the place which the Jew holds in relation to the whole problem of human civilization, we must bear in mind the essential fact that there never has been any Jewish art and consequently that nothing of this kind exists today. We must realize that essentially in those two royal domains of art, namely architecture and music, the Jew has done no original creative work. When the Jew comes to producing something in the field of art he merely bowdlerizes something already in existence or simply steals the intellectual work of others. The Jew essentially lacks those qualities which are characteristic of those creative races that are the founders of civilization.

33. *C. M. Bowra of Oxford University wrote of how German scholars who had fled from Germany had assisted classical studies at Oxford and of the harm done to German scholarship by the Nazis:*

> All these men produced large and learned books and set a high example of research. Our classical school throve through their help, and in the classics, as in other fields, German nationalism defeated its own ends. By expelling some of the best men it gravely impoverished studies which had for two centuries been built up with the highest devotion and integrity.

THE NAZI SENSE OF HISTORY

Nazi thinking was permeated by a strong sense of the German past which was used to bolster the nationalist spirit and to provide Nazism with the sanctity of tradition. (Note also in Extracts 12 and 13 how Hitler was aware that he was playing a large part in the making of contemporary history.)

34. *Hitler shows in this extract from* Mein Kampf *how his school lessons gave him a deep feeling for German history:*

> Probably my whole future life was determined by the fact that I had a professor of history who understood, as few others

understand, how to make this viewpoint prevail in teaching and in examining. This teacher was Dr. Leopold Poetsch, of the Realschule at Linz. He was the ideal personification of the qualities necessary to a teacher of history . . . An elderly gentleman with a decisive manner but a kindly heart, he was a very attractive speaker and was able to inspire us with his own enthusiasm. Even today I cannot recall without emotion that venerable personality whose enthusiastic exposition of history so often made us entirely forget the present and allow ourselves to be transported as if by magic into the past. He penetrated through the dim mist of thousands of years and transformed the historical memory of the dead past into a living reality. When we listened to him we became afire with enthusiasm and we were sometimes moved even to tears.

It was still more fortunate that this professor was able not only to illustrate the past by examples from the present but from the past he was also able to draw a lesson for the present. He understood better than any other the everyday problems that were then agitating our minds. The national fervour which we felt in our own small way was utilized by him as an instrument of our education, in as much as he often appealed to our national sense of honour; for in that way he maintained order and held our attention much more easily than he could have done by any other means. It was because I had such a professor that history became my favourite subject. As a natural consequence, but without the conscious connivance of my professor, I then and there became a young rebel.

35. *Stephen H. Roberts, of the University of Sydney, visited Germany in 1936 and observed Hitler on a number of occasions. Here he emphasizes how enthralled Hitler was with the romantic elements in German history:*

He is a romantic through and through, and he lacks the education or the reading to temper his romanticism by the balance of philosophy. Everything that he does is Wagnerian—this is the *leitmotif* of the whole Hitler piece. He has the trappings of mysticism everywhere. He blesses banners; he makes a workaday shovel a symbol for mysterious ritual; he believes in macabre rites about the resurrection of the Nazi dead; he fosters midnight ceremonies on the sacred Brocken mountain; he talks of Valhalla and knight errantry; he wants to be Siegfried and Frederick the Great rolled into one.

NAZISM AND THE STATE

36. *Before the Nazis came to power Hitler had formed his views on the functions of the State and the Nazi Party and the relationship between them. In* Mein Kampf *he wrote of the State as being a vessel, holding and preserving the dynamic element of race:*

The State is only a means to an end. Its end and its purpose is to preserve and promote a community of human beings who are physically as well as spiritually kindred. Above all, it must preserve the existence of the race, thereby providing the indispensable condition for the free development of all the forces dormant in this race. . . The State is only the vessel and the race is what it contains. The vessel can have a meaning only if it preserves and safeguards the contents. Otherwise it is worthless.

HITLER AND LEADERSHIP

37. *The Nazi belief in the leader-principle* (Führerprinzip), *well in evidence after 1933, stemmed partly from the distaste felt by Germans of the nineteenth century for the determining of policy by the counting of votes. In the person of Hitler the true will of the German people was demonstrated as Ernst Huber, the Nazi political theorist, showed:*

The Führer is the bearer of the people's will; he is independent of all groups, associations, and interests, but he is bound by laws which are inherent in the nature of his people. In this twofold condition: independence of all factional interests but unconditional dependence on the people, is reflected the true nature of the Führer principle . . . He is no 'organ' of the State in the sense of a mere executive agent . . . In his will the will of the people is realized. He transforms the mere feelings of the people into a conscious will . . . Thus it is possible for him, in the name of the true will of the people which he serves, to go against the subjective opinions and convictions of single individuals within the people if these are not in accord with the objective destiny of the people. . . . He shapes the collective will of the people within himself and he embodies the political unity and entirety of the people in opposition to individual interests . . .

38. *The elements of race, the individual's sense of duty and the qualities of leadership are combined in this extract from Hitler's speech to the Reichstag in 1939. It also shows the low priority Hitler gave to intellectual abilities as a component of leadership (see Extract 31):*

Gentlemen, we are faced with further enormous and stupendous tasks. A new reserve of leaders must be formed within our people. Its composition is dependent on race. It is, however, just as necessary to demand and make sure through the system and method of our education, that above all bravery and readiness to accept responsibility should be regarded as essential qualities in those about to assume public office of any kind. When appointing men to leading positions in the State and Party, greater value should be placed on character than on purely academic or allegedly intellectual suitability. It is not abstract knowledge which must be considered a decisive factor wherever a leader is required but rather a natural talent for leadership and with it a highly developed sense of responsibility which brings with it determination, courage and endurance.

39. *Twelve years before that interview Hitler showed that he had already understood how a leader could convince the people of the justice of his cause:*

The art of leadership, as displayed by really great popular leaders in all ages, consists in consolidating the attention of the people against a single adversary and taking care that nothing will split up that attention into sections. The more the militant energies of the people are directed towards one objective the more will new recruits join the movement, attracted by the magnetism of its unified action, and thus the striking power will be all the more enhanced. The leader of genius must have the ability to make different opponents appear as if they belong to the one category; for weak and wavering natures among a leader's following may easily begin to be dubious about the justice of their own cause if they have to face different enemies.

40. *At the same time he laid down the broad lines along which Nazi propaganda was to operate on the political feelings of the masses. In these two extracts he emphasizes the effectiveness of simplicity of statement and, remembering perhaps the teaching of Dr. Poetsch (Extract 34), the need to silence the opposing point of view:*

The receptive powers of the masses are very restricted, and their understanding is feeble. On the other hand, they quickly forget. Such being the case, all effective propaganda must be confined to a few bare essentials and those must be expressed as far as possible in stereotyped formulas. These slogans should be persistently repeated until the very last individual has come to grasp the idea that has been put forward. If this principle be forgotten and if an attempt be made to be abstract and general, the propaganda will turn out ineffective; for the public will not be able to digest or retain what is offered to them in this way. Therefore, the greater the scope of the message that has to be presented, the more necessary it is for the propaganda to discover that plan of action which is psychologically the most efficient.

41. The aim of propaganda is not to try to pass judgment on conflicting rights, giving each its due, but exclusively to emphasize the right which we are asserting. Propaganda must not investigate the truth objectively and, in so far as it is favourable to the other side, present it according to the theoretical rules of justice; but it must present only that aspect of the truth which is favourable to its own side. It was a fundamental mistake to discuss the question of who was responsible for the outbreak of the war and declare that the sole responsibility could not be attributed to Germany. The sole responsibility should have been laid on the shoulders of the enemy, without any discussion whatsoever.

42. *Nazi propaganda was also effective because of the means it exclusively possessed after 1933. Albert Speer, the Nazi Minister for Armaments and War Production, told the court at his trial in Nuremberg of the results of party control of press and radio and gave an acute insight into its implications for leadership:*

Hitler's dictatorship differed in one fundamental point from all its predecessors in history. His was the first dictatorship in the present period of modern technical development, a dictatorship which made complete use of all technical means in a perfect manner for the domination of its own country.

Through technical devices like the radio and the loudspeaker, eighty million people were deprived of independent thought. It was thereby possible to subject them to the will of one man. . .

Earlier dictators needed highly qualified assistants, even at the lowest level, men who could think and act independently. The totalitarian system in the period of modern technical development can dispense with them; the means of communications alone make it possible to mechanize the lower leadership. As a result of this there arises the new type of the uncritical recipient of orders. . . Another result was the far-reaching supervision of the citizens of the State and the maintenance of a high degree of secrecy for criminal acts.

The nightmare of many a man that one day nations could be dominated by technical means was all but realized in Hitler's totalitarian system.

43. *Winston Churchill, however, had given warning in 1934 of the consequences of Nazi control of the means of mass communication:*

This is not the only Germany which we shall live to see, but we have to consider that at present two or three men, in what may well be a desperate position, have the whole of that mighty country in their grip, have that wonderful, scientific, intelligent, docile, valiant people in their grip, a population of 70,000,000 . . . and that there is no public opinion except what is manufactured by those new and terrible engines of broadcasting and a controlled Press.

NAZI RALLIES AS A MEANS OF PROPAGANDA

44. *The Nazis frequently organized mass meetings as part of their propaganda. Stephen H. Roberts wrote of the emotional impact of one meeting upon the gathering and himself:*

The Rally opened in the huge Congress Hall, where 60,000 people gathered to listen to Hitler's proclamation on his achievements of the last three years. Hundreds of swastika banners filed in, to the impressive music of the 'Song of the Standards', and formed a solid mass of red and gold at the back of the stage. Every device of music and coloured light was used to keep the atmosphere tense and the spotlight that played on the giant swastika behind the banners exerted an influence that was almost hypnotic.

The atmosphere was most strained and unreal. The speakers deliberately played on the feelings of the people. At intervals, when something particularly impressive was read out, a curious tremor swept the crowd, and all around me individuals uttered a strange cry, a kind of emotional sigh that invariably changed into a shout of 'Heil Hitler!'. It was a definite struggle to remain rational in a horde so surcharged with tense emotionalism.

45. *William L. Shirer, an American foreign correspondent in Germany from 1934 described a rally held in that year and the willingness of the audience to surrender independence of thought and action:*

'We are strong and will get stronger,' Hitler shouted at them through the microphone, his words echoing across the hushed field from the loudspeakers. And there, in the floodlit night, jammed together like sardines, in one mass formation, the little men of Germany who have made Nazism possible achieved the highest state of being the Germanic man knows: the shedding of their individual souls and minds—with the personal responsibilities and doubts and problems—until under the mystic lights and at the sound of the magic words of the Austrian they were merged completely in the Germanic herd.

46. *Otto Strasser and his brother Gregor broke with Hitler over matters of policy. Otto Strasser, who had stressed the socialist element in Nazism, conveyed in his memoirs the close emotional bond between Hitler and his audience:*

Hitler responds to the vibrations of the human heart with the delicacy of a seismograph, or perhaps of a wireless receiving set, enabling him, with a certainty with which no conscious gift could endow him, to act as a loudspeaker proclaiming the most secret desires, the least admissible instincts, the sufferings and personal revolts of a whole nation.

. . . I have been asked many times what is the secret of Hitler's extraordinary power as a speaker. I can only attribute it to his uncanny intuition, which infallibly diagnoses the ills from which his audience is suffering. If he tries to bolster up his argument with theories or quotations from books he has only imperfectly understood, he scarcely rises above a very poor mediocrity. But let him throw away his crutches and step out boldly, speaking as the spirit moves him, and he is promptly transformed into one of the greatest speakers of the century. . . . Adolf Hitler enters a hall. He snuffs the air. For a minute he gropes, feels his way, senses the atmosphere. Suddenly he bursts forth.

His words go like an arrow to their target, he touches each private wound on the raw, liberating the mass unconscious, expressing its innermost aspirations, telling it what it most wants to hear.

QUESTIONS:

1. Would you agree that the call for action (Extract 15) and the National Socialist programme (Extract 16) both seek the same objectives?
2. In Extracts 17 and 18 Hitler speaks of two forms of German nationalism—his own view of it and that which was widespread before and after the war. How did he distinguish them?
3. What did Hitler consider were the characteristics and achievements of the Aryan race?
4. The Jews were not a threat because of their racial characteristics alone; Hitler also linked them with other powerful forces. What were they?
5. What is the theme of the four extracts, 27 to 30?
6. Why were writers and thinkers considered unfit for leadership? Why did Hitler praise Dr. Poetsch (Extract 34)?
7. Do you see any similarities between Hitler's statements about himself (Extracts 12, 13 and 34) and the observation of him by Roberts (Extract 35)?
8. What was the task of a leader in the Nazi view?
9. What evidence is there of Hitler's insight into the psychology of the people?
10. How important was control of press and radio to the Nazis?
11. What methods were used to sway the emotions of audiences at mass rallies?

3. Hitler—His Life and Personality

HITLER'S EMOTIONAL RESPONSES

47. *There is little doubt that Hitler's personality strongly influenced the fortunes of Germany and the Nazi Party. His own statements and the observations of those who knew him give an insight into his personality. Shirer wrote of the emotional effects of a stimulus upon Hitler's behaviour:*

> For the first time in all the years I've observed him, he seemed tonight to have completely lost control of himself. When he sat down after his talk Goebbels sprang up and shouted: 'One thing is sure: 1918 will never be repeated!' Hitler looked up to him, as if those were the words which he had been searching for all evening. He leaped to his feet and, with a fanatical fire in his eyes that I shall never forget, brought his right hand, after a grand sweep, pounding down on the table, and yelled with all the power in his mighty lungs: 'Ja!' Then he slumped into his chair exhausted.

48. *General Guderian, the Panzer leader, told of Hitler's reaction at the end of a long argument:*

> His fists raised, his cheeks flushed with rage, his whole body trembling, the man stood there in front of me, beside himself with fury and having lost all self-control.
>
> After each outburst of rage Hitler would stride up and down the carpet edge, then suddenly stop immediately before me and hurl his next accusation in my face. He was almost screaming, his eyes seemed about to pop out of his head and the veins stood out on his temples.

HIS SELF-DELUSION

49. *Roberts noted how Hitler believed in himself but also how much he suffered from self-delusion:*

But he is transparently honest. He believes what he is saying, and throws every ounce of nervous energy into all that he says or does, even when he is answering the most casual question (this stands out as my keenest impression when I spoke to him in the Deutscher Hof). Nobody can doubt his utter sincerity. He cannot help himself; he cannot restrain himself. He is completely absorbed in the statement or policy of the moment. That explains why he carries the crowd with him—because he believes so utterly, so appallingly, in what he is saying.

Nevertheless, he can say different things in successive moments and believe in each with the same degree of fervour. It is not his honesty that is in question; it is his terrific power of self-delusion that introduces such an element of uncertainty into everything he does.

HIS SENSE OF HIS OWN GREATNESS

50. *The British Ambassador to Germany, Sir Nevile Henderson, commented on Hitler's growing belief in his own greatness and place in history (Note Extracts 12, 13, 25 and 35):*

When I first met him, his logic and sense of realities had impressed me, but as time went on he appeared to me to become more and more unreasonable and more and more convinced of his own infallibility and greatness. In the end Bismarck was no longer an equal.

HIS VOLUNTARY ISOLATION FROM OTHERS

51. *Ludecke pointed to the way in which Hitler had surrounded himself with a circle within which criticism was unknown and intellectual exchange became impossible:*

The fact that he was always the centre of a spellbound audience explains why for so many years Hitler was unable to listen to anyone or to carry on a normal conversation. In his circle Hitler alone talked; the others listened. . . It gave him a firm foundation for effective speaking; but at the same time his character became set in a mould of intellectual isolation which became one of his weaknesses.

52. *Roberts also remarked on the dangers of Hitler's voluntary isolation:*

Most of his trouble, indeed, seems to be due to his enforced seclusion from mankind. . . He lives in an unnatural detachment that makes his disease of being a godhead batten on itself: the most balanced of human beings could not stand this kind of a life without losing a sense of realities, and nobody would call Hitler emotionally balanced at the best of times. . . Abnormal himself, the constant adulation makes him pathological. He receives only the thrice-distilled views of the lunatics, intriguers and genuine patriots around him. . . He lives in a mental world of his own, more aloof than any Sun-King, and he has only the narrow mental equipment and experience of an agitator to guide him. . . It is the most extraordinary comment on human evolution that, in this age of science and progress, the fate of mankind rests on the whimsy of an abnormal mind, infinitely more so than in the days of the old despots whom we criticize so much.

53. *Otto Strasser not only remarked on Hitler's unwillingness to listen to the views of others but noted how he subordinated the responsibility of power to the desire to gain it. Strasser wrote of a meeting with Hitler in the nineteen-twenties:*

I remember one of my first conversations with him. It was nearly our first quarrel.

'Power!' screamed Adolf. 'We must have power!'

'Before we gain it,' I replied firmly, 'let us decide what we propose to do with it. . .'

Hitler who even then could hardly bear contradiction, thumped the table and barked:

'Power first! Afterwards we can act as circumstances dictate.'

HITLER AND MUSSOLINI

54. *Hitler was an early admirer of Mussolini. He remained loyal to him, and, outwardly at least, a deep respect and affection developed between the two men. In* Mein Kampf *Hitler showed this admiration:*

At that time—I admit it openly—I conceived a profound admiration for that great man beyond the Alps, whose ardent love for his people inspired him not to bargain with Italy's internal enemies but to use all possible ways and means in an effort to wipe them out. What places Mussolini in the ranks of the world's great men is his decision not to share Italy with the Marxists but to redeem his country from Marxism by destroying internationalism.

What miserable pigmies our sham statesmen in Germany appear by comparison with him. And how nauseating it is to witness the conceit and effrontery of these nonentities in criticizing a man who is a thousand times greater than them.

55. *During the tense days of March 1938 when Germany annexed Austria, Hitler was delighted by Mussolini's willingness to accede to his plans. No doubt much of his joy was due to the relief from anxiety which Mussolini's support provided but a close bond of comradeship is evident amidst his effusiveness. Prince Philip of Hesse reported to Hitler:*

Hesse: I have just come back from the Palazzo Venezia. The Duce accepted the whole thing in a very friendly manner. He sends you his regards... Then Mussolini said that Austria is a 'fait accompli' to him.

Hitler: Then please tell Mussolini I will never forget him for this.

Hesse: Yes.

Hitler: Never, never, never, whatever happens... As soon as the Austrian affair is settled, I shall be ready to go with him, through thick and thin, no matter what happens.

Hesse: Yes, my Fuehrer.

Hitler: Listen, I shall make any agreement—I am no longer in fear of the terrible position which would have existed militarily in case we had got into a conflict. You may tell him that I thank him ever so much; never, never shall I forget that.

Hesse: Yes, my Fuehrer.

Hitler: I will never forget, whatever may happen. If he should ever need any help or be in any danger, he can be convinced that I shall stick to him, whatever may happen, even if the whole world were against him.

Hesse: Yes, my Fuehrer.

QUESTIONS:
1. What kinds of stimuli provoked extreme emotion in Hitler?
2. From your reading of Extracts 49 and 50, would you say that Hitler's isolation from others (Extracts 51 and 52) would naturally follow from his self-delusion?
3. What did Hitler admire in Mussolini?

4. The Nazi Consolidation of Power, 1933 - 1935

REICHSTAG ELECTION FIGURES, 1919–1933

56. *1932 was a year of confused politics, intrigue and instability—too complicated to be dealt with here. Briefly, the Nazis suffered a reverse in the November elections, although remaining the largest party. Stable government was impossible, the Chancellor, Schleicher, resigned—and Hitler, correctly judging the situation, placed President Hindenburg in a position where he was obliged to offer the chancellorship to him. Hitler accepted office on January 30th, 1933. The table on the next page indicates something of the instability of German politics during the life of the republic.*

THE NAZIS AND THE ELECTIONS OF MARCH 1933

57. *In February 1933 some of Germany's wealthiest industrialists attended a meeting at which Hitler and Goering urged them to contribute large sums to the party funds for fighting the elections of the following month. Goering revealed the intentions of the Nazis should they be successful and emphasized the need for financial sacrifices which:*

. . .would be much easier for industry to bear if it realized that the election of March 5th will surely be the last one for the next ten years, probably even for the next hundred years.

ELECTIONS FOR THE REICHSTAG 1919-1933

Party	Jan. 1919	June 1920	May 1924	Dec. 1924	May 1928	Sept. 1930	July 1932	Nov. 1932	March 1933
Social Democratic	163	113	100	131	152	143	133	121	120
Independent Socialist	22	18	—	—	—	—	—	—	—
Communist	—	2	62	45	54	77	89	100	81
Catholic Centre	71	68	65	69	61	68	75	70	73
Bavarian Peoples'	18	19	16	19	17	19	22	20	19
Hanoverian	3	4	5	4	3	3	—	1	—
Peoples'	22	62	44	51	45	30	7	11	2
Democrat	74	44	28	32	25	14	4	2	5
Economic	—	—	9	17	23	23	2	1	—
Independents	4	4	5	—	—	51	7	10	6
Nationalist	42	65	106	103	79	41	40	51	53
National Socialist	—	—	32	14	13	107	230	196	288
TOTAL	419	462	472	485	472	576	609	583	647

1. Candidates were elected on the proportional representation system which gave the smaller parties a chance to win seats.
2. The number of seats was determined by the total number of votes cast in each election.

THE BURNING OF THE REICHSTAG

58. *Before the March elections took place the Nazis strove to discredit their political opponents and influence the voters against them. One of the events they used for propaganda purposes against the Communists was the burning down of the Reichstag buildings.*
The Times *reported on the event:**

A communication about the Reichstag fire was issued by the Prussian authorities this morning. . . It gives an illuminating glimpse into the state of mind prevailing in official Germany today.

'This act of incendiarism [it says] is the most outrageous act yet committed by Bolshevism in Germany. Among the masses of subversive literature, which the police found during their search of the Karl Liebknecht House, were instructions for a Communist-terrorist outbreak on Bolshevist lines. According to this, Government buildings, palaces, museums, and essential public undertakings were to be set on fire. . . The discovery of this material has upset the plans for effecting a Bolshevist revolution. The burning of the Reichstag, however, was to have been the signal for a bloody uprising and civil war. For four o'clock on Tuesday morning widespread plunderings in Berlin had been organized. It is established that today acts of terrorism were to have begun all over Germany against individuals, against private property, and against the lives of peaceful citizens, and that a general civil war was to have started.'

59. *In the same edition it summarized the decree of Hitler, promulgated on February 28th, the day after the fire, which, as it stated, was designed to end Communist violence:*

The decree . . . consists of two main clauses.

The first suspends all Articles of the Constitution relating to the liberty of the person, freedom of expression, of the Press and of assembly. . .

The second clause provides that if any German Federal State does not take the necessary measures under the decree for the preservation of public order and security the Reich Government can displace its executive and take over the direction of its affairs.

* See article by A. J. P. Taylor in *History Today*, August 1961, for a study of the propaganda use made by the Nazis of the Reichstag fire.

60. *The Nazis charged a young Dutchman with burning down the Reichstag in order to establish that his act was part of a plan for Communist terrorism throughout Germany. The* Times *quoted the words of a prominent German socialist who disclaimed knowledge of the Dutchman:*

> As Herr Stampfer, the Socialist deputy and editor of the suppressed *Vorwärts*, points out, the only evidence adduced that the party had any connection with the firing of the Reichstag is that a young man, entirely unknown in Social-Democratic circles, who is said to have started the fire with the aid of his own shirt . . . has stated that he stood in some relation or other to the Socialist Party.

THE ENABLING ACT

61. *Within a month the Reichstag had passed the Enabling Act which gave Hitler arbitrary power for four years. Using the decree of February 28th as a threat and being able to leave the eighty-one Communist deputies out of the reckoning he conciliated the Centre Party and gained the necessary two-thirds majority in the Reichstag. The* Times *reported Hitler's speech to the Reichstag:*

> It would contradict the spirit of the national resurgence, said the Chancellor, if the Government had to bargain and beg for the approval of the Reichstag for each and every one of its actions, and for this reason they needed the Enabling Bill. They did not intend to abandon the Reichstag. . .
>
> The number of cases in which recourse must be had to such a Bill is limited; but the Government insists the more firmly that it be passed. The Government will regard its rejection as a declaration of resistance. Now, gentlemen, you may yourselves decide for peace or war.

62. *The newspaper left no doubt on what it thought about German parliamentary procedure as the vote was being taken on the Bill:*

> The 'drill parade' then began. Captain Göring, the Nazi speaker, told assenting Deputies to stand up and in this way the second and third readings were passed in a matter of seconds. A card vote then confirmed the result. The *Reichsrat* met immediately after and approved the Enabling Bill without debate.

63. *One day later it showed the same scorn and pointed out the lack of resistance to Hitler:*

President von Hindenburg today signed the Enabling Bill, which was immediately promulgated, and therewith was completed the process by which the legislative power in Germany is vested in Herr Hitler for four years. 'Politics in seven-league boots' is an apt Nationalist description for the rapid drafting, approval by both legislative bodies, and promulgation of the Bill on which 'the New Germany' is to be built up; and the Nationalist Press again contemplates happily the smart way in which the parties, drilled from the Chair, went through the motions of legislation. The Press, like Parliament, is strictly disciplined, and comment is as rare as interjection.

THE TRADE UNIONS

64. *The Gestapo was formed in April and armed with this coercive power to silence opposition, Hitler turned his attention to the labour movement. The day before trade unions were declared illegal, Hitler gave a hint of their future rôle:*

... The unification of the German Workmen's Movement has a great moral significance. When we complete the reconstruction of the State, which must be the result of very great concessions on both sides, we want to have two parties to the contract facing each other who both are in their hearts on principle nationally minded, who both look only to their people, and who both on principle are ready to subordinate everything else in order to serve the common weal.

65. *On that day, May 2nd, while union leaders were being arrested, Robert Ley, who was given control of the Nazi Labour Front, proclaimed:*

Workers! Your institutions are sacred to us National Socialists. I myself am a poor peasant's son and understand poverty, I myself was seven years in one of the biggest industries in Germany and I know the exploitation of anonymous capitalism. Workers! I swear to you we will not only keep everything which exists, we will build up the protection and rights of the workers even further.

THE SILENCING OF POLITICAL OPPOSITION

66. *In July 1933 Hitler declared all political opposition to be illegal:*

The German Government has enacted the following law, which is herewith promulgated:

Article I: The National Socialist German Workers' Party constitutes the only political Party in Germany.

Article II: Whoever undertakes to maintain the organizational structure of another political Party or to form a new political Party will be punished with penal servitude up to three years or with imprisonment up to three years, if the action is not subject to a greater penalty according to other regulations.

The Reich Chancellor,
ADOLF HITLER

HITLER AND THE CHURCHES

67. *In that month also the Protestant groups were obliged to accept a new constitution which rapidly became the means of forcing the Church under State Control. (See also Extracts 72 and 73.) The Roman Catholic Church, despite the Concordat of July 20th, lost much of its authority. But in the preceding March Hitler, in order to gain the support of the Catholic Centre Party for the passage of the Enabling Bill, had declared:*

The rights of the Churches will not be diminished, and their relationship to the State will not be modified.

68. *Having secured the superiority of the State in religious matters Hitler made these remarks on the Roman Catholic Church in 1936:*

... I know ... how to handle the Church. If she will not accommodate herself to us, I will let loose upon her a propaganda that will exceed her powers of healing and of sight. I will set in motion against her the Press, the wireless, and the film.... I know how to handle these fellows and how they are to be caught out. They shall bend or break—but, since they are no fools, they will bow their heads.

THE ELIMINATION OF THE S.A.

69. *By 1934, the S.A. had become an obstacle to Hitler's plans. Further-more this private Nazi army was regarded as a serious challenge by the Army itself. Detailed evidence is lacking but it seems quite certain that in April Hitler and the Army came to terms—the Army was to swear its allegiance to Hitler upon the death of the ageing President Hindenburg in return for which Hitler was to eliminate the S.A. Three months before this secret agreement, Hitler wrote to Ernst Roehm, an old friend and chief of the S.A.:*

My dear Chief of Staff,
The fight of the National Socialist Movement and the National Socialist Revolution were rendered possible for me by the consistent suppression of the Red Terror by the S.A. If the Army has to guarantee the protection of the nation against the world beyond our frontiers, the task of the S.A. is to secure the victory of the National Socialist Revolution and the existence of the National Socialist State and the community of our people in the domestic sphere. When I summoned you to your present position, my dear Chief of Staff, the S.A. was passing through a serious crisis. It is primarily due to your services if, after a few years, this political instrument could develop that force which enabled me to face the final struggle for power and to succeed in laying low the Marxist opponent.
At the close of the year of the National Socialist Revolution, therefore, I feel compelled to thank you, my dear Ernst Roehm, for the imperishable services which you have rendered to the National Socialist Movement and the German people, and to assure you how very grateful I am to Fate that I am able to call such men as you my friends and fellow-combatants.
In true friendship and grateful regard,
Your ADOLF HITLER

70. *On the night of June 30th the blow fell. Senior S.A. officers, inclu-ding Roehm, were murdered and on July 13th Hitler spoke to the Reichstag, explaining his reasons for the action:*

At the beginning of June ... I assured the Chief of Staff, Roehm, that the assertion that the S.A. was to be dissolved was an infamous lie and that I refused to make any comment upon the lie that I myself intended to attack the S.A.

71. *The following extracts from the same speech reveal his thoughts after he had reached agreement with the Army:*

In the State there is only one bearer of arms, and that is the Army; there is only one bearer of the political will, and that is the National Socialist Party... If during these months I hesitated again and again before taking a final decision that was due to two considerations:

1. I could not lightly persuade myself to believe that a relation which I thought to be founded on loyalty could be only a lie.
2. I still always cherished the secret hope that I might be able to spare the Movement and my S.A. the shame of such a dis-agreement. . . .

THE NUREMBERG LAWS

72. *On September 15th, 1935, Hitler took his first action to deprive the Jews of German citizenship. These Nuremberg Laws, which also forbade marriage between Germans and Jews, opened the way for racial persecution in following years. The day after the laws were passed the* New York Times *cited Hitler's speech at Nuremberg:*

In order to reach an amicable relation between the German people and the Jews, the Government will try to bring about legal regulation. The law ... constitutes only an attempt at legal regulation. However, should this not work we will have to take it up once again. If Jewish agitation within and without Germany continues we will then examine the situation again.

QUESTIONS:
1. Why was Goering so sure that his prophecy would be well received by the industrialists (Extract 57)?
2. What is the view of *The Times* concerning the Reichstag fire (Extracts 58 to 60)?
3. Why was the Enabling Bill passed so easily in the Reichstag (Extracts 61 to 63)?
4. What 'hint of the future rôle' of trade unions is to be found in Extract 64?

5. Would you regard the decree banning political parties (Extract 66) as being one of the more important pieces of Nazi legislation?

6. If Hitler was determined to bend religion to his will (Extract 68), why did he declare to the world that he had never interfered with its rights (Extract 73)?

7. Read Extracts 69 to 71 carefully and try to follow Hitler's theme from January 1934 (the letter to Roehm) to July 1934 (the speech in the Reichstag). Do you believe Hitler was working to a plan?

8. Why is Hitler at pains to soften the blow of the Nuremberg Laws in his speech (Extract 72)?

5. Domestic Policy, 1933 - 1939

NAZI CONTROL OVER THE CHURCHES

73. *Church–State relationships worsened during the thirties. At first the Nazis attempted to identify National Socialism with Christianity but later declared the two beliefs to be irreconcilable. In 1939, Hitler illustrated the extent of State control over religion:*

I should only like to ask this question:

What sums have France, England or America paid to their Churches through the State within the same period of time?

The National-Socialist State has neither closed any Church nor prevented any service from being held, nor has it ever influenced the form of a church service. It has neither interfered with the doctrinal teaching nor with the creed of any denomination. But, of course, the National-Socialist State allows anybody to serve God as he chooses.

But: The National-Socialist State will ruthlessly make clear to those clergy who instead of being God's ministers regard it as their mission to speak insultingly of our present Reich, its organizations or its leaders, that no one will tolerate a destruction of this State, and that clergy who place themselves beyond the pale of the Law will be called to account before the Law like any other German citizen. Let it be mentioned, however, that there are tens of thousands of clergy of all Christian denominations who fulfil their ecclesiastical duties just as well or probably better than the political agitators, without ever coming into conflict with the laws of the State. The State considers their protection its task. The destruction of the enemies of the State is its duty.

74. *Alfred Rosenberg not only emphasized the superiority of a State-controlled Church but introduced severe limitations on its religious authority:*

1. The National Reich Church specifically demands the immediate turning over to its possession of all churches and chapels, to become national churches.

7. In the National Reich Church . . . only the national 'orators of the Reich' will be allowed to speak.

10. The National Reich Church will unceasingly pursue its efforts to attach itself to the State, to which it will submit as a loyal servant.

18. The National Reich Church will remove from the altars of all churches the Bible, the cross and religious objects.

19. In their place will be set . . . our most saintly book, *Mein Kampf*, and to the left of this a sword.

NAZI EDUCATION

75. *The Nazis clearly saw religion and the schools as opponents of its ideology and Stephen Roberts, in 1936, noted the triumph of Nazi power over religion and education:*

Again and again in Germany, even in Catholic Bavaria and the Black Forest, I found cases of children whose Roman Catholic parents tried to keep them in the few struggling Church societies that still existed for children. In every case the children wanted to join the Hitler *Jugend*. . . To be outside Hitler's organization was the worst form of punishment. . . I have seen groups of boys in their teens gaping almost with idolatry at one of their fellows who had been singled out for a salute from Baldur von Schirach; and I soon learnt not to answer the children's stock query: 'Have you seen the Führer?' by answering 'Yes, and I have spoken with him.' The resultant worship was too distressing. Their attitude of mind is absolutely uncritical. They do not see in Hitler a statesman with good and bad points; to them he is more than a demigod . . . It is this utter lack of any objective or critical attitude on the part of youth, even with university students, that made me fear most for the future of Germany. They are nothing but vessels for State propaganda, and the copious draught allows no time for thought, even if they had not lost the habit.

76. *Hitler often affirmed the influence of his teacher, Dr. Poetsch, on his thinking and in* Mein Kampf *he foresaw the need for National Socialism to implant racial attitudes:*

The whole organization of education and training which the People's State is to build up must take as its crowning task the work of instilling into the hearts and brains of the youth entrusted to it the racial instincts and understanding of the racial idea. No boy or girl must leave school without having attained a clear insight into the meaning of racial purity and the importance of maintaining the racial blood unadulterated. Thus the first indispensable condition for the preservation of our race will have been established and thus the future cultural progress of our people will be assured.

HITLER'S ATTITUDE TO THE LAW

77. *Nazi disregard of the Law was evident long before the nineteen-thirties (e.g. Extracts 16 and 54). This contempt for justice was revealed by Goering in a speech two days before the March 1933 elections:*

Fellow Germans, my measures will not be crippled by any judicial thinking. My measures will not be crippled by any bureaucracy. Here I don't have to worry about Justice, my mission is only to destroy and exterminate, nothing more. This struggle will be a struggle against chaos, and such a struggle I shall not conduct with the power of the police. A bourgeois State might have done that. Certainly, I shall use the power of the State and the police to the utmost, my dear Communists, so don't draw any false conclusions; but the struggle to the death, in which my fist will grasp your necks, I shall lead with those down there—the Brown Shirts.

78. *The electoral laws contained in the Weimar Constitution were ignored at lower levels also:*

Copy is attached enumerating the persons who cast 'No' votes or invalid votes at Kappel. The control was effected in the following way: some members of the election committee marked all the ballots with numbers. During the balloting a voters' list was made up. The ballots were handed out in numerical order, therefore it was possible afterward . . . to find out the persons who cast 'No' votes or invalid votes. The marking was done on the back of the ballot with skimmed milk.

79. *In his Reichstag speech of July 1933 (see Extracts 70 and 71) in which he gave details of his action against the S.A., Hitler explained why the courts could not have been used to resolve the crisis:*

If anyone reproaches me and asks why I did not resort to the regular courts of justice for conviction of the offender, then all that I can say to him is this: in this hour I was responsible for the fate of the German people, and thereby I became the supreme Justiciar of the German people!

Everyone must know for all future time that if he raises his hand to strike the State, then certain death is his lot.

80. *Under the power of decree granted Hitler by the Enabling Act (see Extracts 61 and 63) a person's arrest was no longer the prerogative of the courts:*

Order for Protective Custody. Based on Article 1 of the decree of the Reich President for the Protection of People and State of February 28th, 1933, you are taken into protective custody in the interest of public security and order.

Reason: Suspicion of activities inimical toward the State.

ECONOMIC INDICES

	National Income (Milliard RM.)	Wholesale Prices 1913 = 100	Industrial Production 1928 = 100	Imports (Mrd. RM.)	Exports (Mrd. RM.)	Employment (000's)	Unemployment (000's)	Currency Circulation (Mrd. RM.)
1928	75·4	140·0	100·0	14·0	12·3	18,000	1,353	5·8
1932	45·2	96·5	58·0	4·7	5·7	12,580	5,575	5·8
1933	46·6	93·3	65·7	4·2	4·9	13,080	4,804	5·4
1934	52·7	98·4	82·9	4·5	4·2	15,090	2,718	5·5
1935	58·6	101·8	95·3	4·2	4·3	16,000	2,151	5·8
1936	65·0	104·1	107·8	4·2	4·8	17,140	1,592	6·2
1937	71·0	105·9	118·8	5·5	5·9	18,370	912	6.7
March 1938	—	105·8	124·6	—	—	18,831	508	7·0

GERMAN ECONOMIC RECOVERY

81. *Germany's economic revival is often regarded as the greatest achievement of the Nazis. The statistics on page 48 indicate the nature and
extent of the recovery.*

82. *C. W. Guillebaud, a Cambridge University lecturer in economics,
visited Germany and wrote on its economic recovery:*

No one who is acquainted with German conditions would
suggest that the standard of living is a high one, but the important
thing is that it has been rising in recent years, and that the attitude
of a people towards their standard of living . . . is very different
according as it represents an improvement or a deterioration on
what they have experienced in the recent past . . .

By the autumn of 1936 the success of the First Four-Year
Plan was no longer in doubt. Unemployment had ceased to be
a serious problem and there was practically full employment in
the building and engineering industries. The national income was
rising steadily and . . . had reached the level of the boom year of
1928; industry and the banking system were fully liquid and
savings were coming forward increasingly in the capital market.
Thus the economic circuit had been closed and the seemingly
hazardous policy which was embarked on in 1932–33 had been
vindicated by the result . . .

When it is remembered that in March 1938 Germany was in a
state of full employment (in the usual sense of this term), that
there was an extreme scarcity of labour, and that many of her most
important industries were working to capacity, with heavy over-
time, this relative stabilization of wages and prices must be regarded as a very remarkable achievement. It is certainly unique
in economic history down to the present time.

ANTI-SEMITISM

83. *In the latter half of the thirties, many visitors to Germany showed
an uneasiness at the mounting persecution of the Jews. Stephen
Roberts wrote of an experience which shows how obsessed one particular German was with the presence of Jews within the Third Reich:*

R— D

A few weeks ago I was being shown around a famous collection of party relics in Munich. The curator was a mild old man, a student of the old German academic class. After showing me everything, he led, almost with bated breath, to his *pièce de résistance*. He produced a small sculptured wooden gibbet from which was suspended a brutally realistic figure of a dangling Jew. This piece of humourless sadism, he said, decorated the table at which Hitler founded the Party, seventeen years ago. Asked if it were not funny, I replied that it was very, very tragic. Sobered for a moment, he replied, and this showed how far apart are the average German and British mental processes. 'That is true. It is tragic—tragic to think what a hold Jewry had on Germany before the Führer came!' The horror of the gross little gibbet and all it signified completely passed him by.

84. *C. M. Bowra has acquainted us with the anti-Semitism of another German and went on to assert that Herr Meyer's racial feelings were shared by others who had helped Hitler to gain power:*

Frau Meyer's husband, who was an unsuccessful lawyer, had strong leanings towards [the Nazis] and aired his views to me. He insisted first that Hitler would restore the pre-1914 frontiers, next that he would put the Jews in their place, and on this he was rabid. He wanted a scapegoat for his own failure, and in the Jews, among whom were many lawyers, he found something made to his hand. . . It was useless to argue with him, as he merely repeated himself and was beyond any appeal to reason. Herr Meyer was not a full-blown Nazi, but he was a characteristic German of the kind which voted Hitler into power and found in him a voice for its own grievances.

85. *There is little point in recounting the mass murder and persecution of Jews within and outside Germany between 1933 and 1945. The total number murdered has been variously estimated at between four and six millions. Possibly the following well-known extract from the testimony of the Commandant of Auschwitz Extermination Camp will serve to illustrate two points—that anti-Semitism inevitably resulted in genocide (Hitler's 'final solution') and that not only was the 'solution' a vast undertaking but that it was possible only in a nation where all authority was vested in the hands of a few:*

The 'final solution' of the Jewish question meant the complete extermination of all Jews in Europe. I was ordered to establish extermination facilities at Auschwitz in June 1941. At that time there were already three other extermination camps in the Government-General: Belzek, Treblinka and Wolzek. I visited Treblinka to find out how they carried out their extermination. The Camp Commandant told me that he had liquidated eighty thousand in the course of one half year. He was principally concerned with liquidating all the Jews from the Warsaw ghetto. He used monoxide gas and I did not think that his methods were very efficient. So at Auschwitz I used Cyclon B, which was a crystallized prussic acid dropped into the death chamber. It took from three to fifteen minutes to kill the people in the chamber, according to climatic conditions. We knew when the people were dead because their screaming stopped. We usually waited about half an hour before we opened the doors and removed the bodies. After the bodies were removed, our special commandos took off the rings and extracted the gold from the teeth of the corpses. Another improvement that we made over Treblinka was that we built our gas-chambers to accommodate two thousand people at one time. . .

QUESTIONS:
1. Extracts 74 and 75 present two methods used by the Nazis to limit the authority of the churches. Which do you consider might have been the more effective?
2. The introduction to Extract 76 speaks of Dr. Poetsch. Are the benefits Hitler gained from his teaching (see Extract 34) the same benefits that he wished to arise from a Nazi system of education?
3. If Hitler was the supreme legislative authority by virtue of the Enabling Act, why did he conceal the illegality of his actions in 1938 (see Extract 78)?
4. What aspects of Germany's economic recovery after 1933 were of significance to the workers (Extracts 81 and 82)?
5. Do the curator (Extract 83) and Herr Meyer (Extract 84) share the same views about the Jews?

6. Foreign Policy, 1933 - 1939

HITLER'S VIEWS ON WAR

86. *Herman Rauschning, one of the early Nazi leaders, wrote this fragment of a conversation with Hitler early in 1934:*

'Do you seriously intend to fight the West?' I asked.
He stopped and looked at me.
'What else do you think we're arming for?' he retorted. . . 'We must proceed step by step, so that no one will impede our advance. How to do this I don't yet know. But that it will be done is guaranteed by Britain's lack of firmness and France's internal disunity.'

87. *Two years later Stephen Roberts told of what he thought to be the direction in which Germany was moving:*

The whole teaching of Hitlerism is to justify war as an instrument of policy . . . and there is hardly a boy in Germany who does not view the preparation for ultimate war as the most important aspect of his life . . . Hitlerism cannot achieve its aims without war; its ideology is that of war . . . Hitler has worked up Germany to such a state that the people are ready to accept war at any moment.

88. *Early in 1939 Hitler in a speech to the Reichstag declared that war was not Germany's intention and that fears of war stemmed from a campaign of international warmongering:*

We believe that if the Jewish international campaign of hatred by press and propaganda could be checked, good understanding could very quickly be established between the peoples. It is only such elements that hope steadfastly for a war. I however believe in a long peace! For in what way do the interests of England and Germany, for example, conflict? I have stated over and over, again and again, that there is no German, and above all no National-Socialist, who even in his most secret thoughts has the intention of causing the British Empire any kind of difficulties. From England, too, the voices of men who think reasonably and calmly, express a similar attitude with regard to Germany. It would be a blessing for the whole world if mutual confidence and co-operation could be established between the two peoples. The same is true of our relations with France.

GERMANY, THE LEAGUE OF NATIONS, AND DISARMAMENT

89. *As Hitler became more confident of Germany's recovery in the nineteen-thirties he voiced with increasing frequency the humiliating and unequal status accorded Germany under the Treaty of Versailles. He took action in October 1933 to declare Germany's unwillingness to remain a second class power:*

In spite of our readiness to carry through German disarmament at any time, if necessary, to its ultimate consequences, other governments could not decide to redeem the pledges signed by them in the Peace Treaty.

By the deliberate refusal of real moral and material equality of rights to Germany, the German nation and its Governments have been profoundly humiliated.

After the German Government had declared that it was again prepared to take part in the Disarmament Conference, the German Foreign Minister and our delegates were informed by the official representatives of other States in public speeches and direct statements that this equality of rights could no longer be granted to present-day Germany.

As the German Government regards this action as an unjust and humiliating discrimination against the German nation, it is not in a position to continue, as an outlawed and second-class nation, to take part in negotiations which could only lead to further arbitrary results.

While the German Government again proclaims its unshaken desire for peace, it declares to its great regret that, in view of these imputations, it must leave the Disarmament Conference. It will also announce its departure from the League of Nations.

GERMAN OCCUPATION OF THE RHINELAND

90. *A part of the Versailles Treaty was the demilitarization of the Rhineland. On February 27th, 1936, France ratified an agreement between it and the Soviet Union after months of bitter controversy in French politics. Hitler was aware of these divisions, Britain's suspicion of the agreement and the probability that the League would not act. The German High Command was alarmed at Hitler's order to send troops into the Rhineland because of Germany's marked military inferiority to France. Proclaiming that the Franco-Soviet Treaty was a threat to German security, Hitler took the gamble and ordered his impudently small force to march. The gamble succeeded and a week later the German Government explained that the military occupation was an attempt to gain peace in Europe. The Times reported on this official announcement:*

What the German Government is striving for is not the conclusion of treaties which, through their being bound up with moral burdens for an honour-loving and decent people, inwardly and outwardly remain incredible, but the bringing about of a real and actual pacification of Europe for the next quarter of a century; in fact a peace . . . based on the free decisions of European nations and States with equal rights.

THE ANTI-COMINTERN PACT

91. *Within quick succession two treaties were signed in late 1936. Germany and Italy signed a treaty of alliance (the Rome–Berlin Axis) and, with Japan, both signed the Anti-Comintern Agreement. This anti-Communist pact was seen by Hitler as a rallying-point for other powers to resist the spread of Communism:*

The Anti-Comintern Pact will perhaps one day become the crystallization point of a group of powers whose ultimate aim is none other than to eliminate the menace to the peace and culture instigated by a satanic apparition. The Japanese nation which in the last two years has set us so many examples of glorious heroism is undoubtedly fighting in the service of civilization . . .

54

GERMAN OCCUPATION OF AUSTRIA

92. *The thirties were a period of great and growing international tension.*
One threat to European peace was Hitler's occupation of Austria,
which took place in 1938. Five years before, a German spokesman
announced on Hitler's behalf:

... By order of Herr Hitler I declare ... that we shall have
attained our goal only when all Germany, including German-
Austria, is united with the Fatherland in one great State that can
thus serve Germany's world mission.

93. *One of the more interesting documents of this decade is the Hossbach*
Minutes, named after Hitler's adjutant. The minutes, which were
revealed at the Nuremberg Trials after the war, record the business
at a secret meeting in November 1937 of Hitler, four of his most
senior service officers and the Foreign Minister. The meeting discussed
two main points—Germany's security and living-space. From these
themes followed Hitler's declared belief that the problem of living-
space must be solved by 1943–1945 when German power would be
at its greatest. But he also declared that security and living-space
could be gained on Germany's southern and eastern flanks before
1943. Clearly Hitler's views had not changed since he wrote Mein
Kampf.
Despite the Austro-German Agreement of July 1936 which recog-
nized Austrian sovereignty, Hitler limited Chancellor Schuschnigg's
ability to preserve Austrian independence by supporting the Austrian
Nazis and charging Schuschnigg with the terrorization of the German
minority. Schuschnigg announced a plebiscite to allow the Austrian
people to vote on the form of government they desired and two days
later, on March 11th, 1938, Hitler, fearing an unfavourable vote,
ordered his troops to cross into Austria. In this speech of March 18th,
Hitler gives reasons for his action:

On Tuesday, 8th March, the first statements reached me about
a plan for a plebiscite. These statements appeared so fantastic
and untrustworthy that they were regarded as mere rumours.
Then on the evening of Wednesday, through a truly astounding
speech, we were informed of an attack not only on the terms
agreed upon between us but more than that—an attack upon the
majority of the Austrian people ... Herr Schuschnigg ... sought
through an unexampled election fraud to create for himself the
moral justification for an open violation of the obligations to

which he had agreed. He wished to gain a mandate for a further and still more brutal oppression of the overwhelming majority of the German-Austrian people.

GERMAN OCCUPATION OF CZECHOSLOVAKIA

94. *In September 1938 the Munich Agreement was signed between Germany, France, Britain and Italy—but without the presence of Czechoslovakia. The agreement allowed Hitler to occupy Sudetenland, part of Czechoslovakia which had a German population. The Czechs felt betrayed by the two western powers. Five months later, on March 14th, 1939, Hitler annexed the whole of Czechoslovakia. He gave, in this proclamation to the German people, similar reasons for occupation to those he had given for the march on Austria one year earlier:*

They will disarm the terrorist bands and the Czech forces which are supporting them, they will protect all those whose lives are threatened, and they will thus secure the basis for the introduction of a fundamental settlement which will do justice to the traditions formed by a thousand years of history and to the practical needs of the German and Czech peoples.

A BRITISH VIEW OF HITLER'S FOREIGN POLICY

95. *In these three extracts from a speech by Lord Halifax, the British Foreign Secretary, to the House of Lords on March 20th, 1939, there is an attempt to justify Britain's part in the Munich Agreement and an uneasiness that Hitler was embarking on a policy of expansion into non-German territories:*

My Lords, the Munich Settlement, which was approved by this House and in another place, was accepted by His Majesty's Government for two purposes, quite distinct. The first purpose was to effect a settlement of a problem which was a real one, and of which the treatment was an urgent necessity if the peace of Europe was to be preserved. As to that, I would say, as I have said before in this House, that I have no doubt whatever that His Majesty's Government were right, in the light of all the information available to them, to take the course they did. The second purpose of Munich was to build a Europe more secure, upon the basis of freely accepted consultation as the means by which all future differences might be adjusted; and that long-term purpose has been, as we have come to observe, disastrously belied by events. We are charged with having too readily believed the assurances which were given by Herr Hitler—that after Munich he had no further territorial ambitions, and no desire to incorporate non-German elements in the Reich.

96. It is no doubt the case that previous assurances had been broken, whatever justification might have been advanced by Herr Hitler, on the grounds of his mission, as he conceives it, to incorporate ex-German territory and predominantly German areas in the Reich. But in his actions until after Munich a case could be made that Herr Hitler had been true to his own principles, the union of Germans in, and the exclusion of non-Germans from, the Reich. Those principles he has now overthrown, and in including eight million Czechs under German rule he has surely been untrue to his own philosophy ... and whatever may have been the truth about the treatment of 250,000 Germans, it is impossible for me to believe that it could only be remedied by the subjugation of eight million Czechs.

97. What conclusions ... are we to draw from this conquest of Czechoslovakia? Are we to believe that German policy has thus entered upon a new phase? Is German policy any longer to be limited to the consolidation of territory predominantly inhabited by persons of German race? Or is German policy now to be directed towards domination over non-German peoples? These are very grave questions which are being asked in all parts of the world today. The German action in Czechoslovakia has been furthered by new methods, and the world has lately seen more than one new departure in the field of international technique. Wars without declarations of war. Pressure exercised under threat of immediate employment of force. Intervention in the internal struggles of other States.

GERMAN–POLISH RELATIONS

98. *In January 1934 Germany and Poland concluded a Non-Aggression Pact which was intended to last for ten years. It eased tension in Europe and was frequently cited by Hitler as a proof of his peaceful intentions as this speech of January 1939 shows:*

We have just celebrated the fifth anniversary of the conclusion of our Non-Aggression Pact with Poland. There can scarcely be any difference of opinion today among true friends of peace with regard to the value of this agreement. One only needs to ask oneself what might have happened to Europe, if this agreement, which brought such relief, had not been entered into five years ago. In signing it, the great Polish Marshal and patriot (Pilsudski) rendered his people just as great a service as the leaders of the National-Socialist State rendered the German people. During the troubled months of the past year, the friendship between Germany and Poland was one of the reassuring factors in the political life of Europe.

99. *But eight months later he condemned the Versailles Treaty for stripping Germany of the port of Danzig and granting a large area of eastern Germany to Poland (the Polish Corridor). His other claim in this speech had become familiar to many:*

For months we have been suffering under the torture of a problem which the Versailles Diktat created—a problem which has deteriorated until it becomes intolerable for us. Danzig was and is a German city. The Corridor was and is German. Both these territories owe their cultural development exclusively to the German people. Danzig was separated from us, the Corridor was annexed by Poland. As in other German territories of the East, all German minorities living there have been ill-treated in the most distressing manner. More than 1,000,000 people of German blood had in the years 1919–1920 to leave their homeland.

THE GERMAN–SOVIET TREATY (1939)

100. *German–Soviet relations in the thirties went through two phases—German opposition to Communism (see Extract 91) and later the*

growth of an uneasy friendship which culminated in the Non-Aggression Treaty of August 23rd, 1939. This extract deals with four of the major clauses:

Article I
Both High Contracting Parties obligate themselves to desist from any act of violence, any aggressive action, and any attack on each other, either individually or jointly with other powers.

Article II
Should one of the High Contracting Parties become the object of belligerent action by a third power, the other High Contracting Party shall in no manner lend its support to this third power.

Article IV
Neither of the two High Contracting Parties shall participate in any grouping of powers whatsoever that is directly or indirectly aimed at the other party.

Article V
Should disputes or conflicts arise between the High Contracting Parties over problems of one kind or another, both parties shall settle these disputes or conflicts exclusively through friendly exchange of opinion or, if necessary, through the establishment of arbitration commissions.

THE BRITISH PRIME MINISTER'S BROADCAST TO THE GERMAN PEOPLE

101. *Germany invaded Poland on September 1st, 1939, and Britain and France went to war against Germany. One day after Britain's declaration of September 3rd her Prime Minister, Neville Chamberlain, broadcast to the German people:*

He gave his word that he would respect the Locarno Treaty; he broke it. He gave his word that he neither wished nor intended to annex Austria; he broke it. He declared that he would not incorporate the Czechs in the Reich; he did so. He gave his word after Munich that he had no further territorial demands in Europe;

he broke it. He gave his word that he wanted no Polish provinces; he broke it. He has sworn to you for years that he was the mortal enemy of Bolshevism; he is now its ally.

Can you wonder his word is, for us, not worth the paper it is written on?

QUESTIONS:

1. Was Germany's withdrawal from the Disarmament Conference and the League of Nations (Extract 89) the action of a country sincerely interested in preserving peace? (Note also Extract 90).

2. By what reasoning did the German Government conclude that the interests of European peace could be served by its order to occupy the Rhineland?

3. Why was Japan invited to be a signatory to the Anti-Comintern Pact?

4. Would the British Foreign Secretary (see Extract 96) have sympathized with the sentiments expressed in Extract 92?

5. Hitler gives a similar reason for Germany's occupation of Austria, Czechoslovakia and Poland (Introductions and Extracts 93, 94 and 99). What is this reason?

6. In Extract 95 the British Foreign Secretary is defending his government's foreign policy which came to be known as 'appeasement'. Does he admit the failure of this policy?

7. He stated that Germany was using 'new methods' in its foreign relations (Extract 97). What were they? Do you believe from your reading of the documents in this section that he was right?

8. Why should Hitler have signed a treaty with the Soviet Union? Do you see any significance in his timing?

9. Is the British Prime Minister (Extract 101), in effect, making the same statement as his Foreign Secretary (see Extract 95)?.

10. It is easy enough to believe that planning in the event of war is the same as intending to make war. Bearing this in mind, read the documents in this section and consider whether it was Hitler's intention in the thirties to make war. (Note especially Extracts 86, 87, 88, 96 and the introduction to Extract 92).

Sources of Extracts

Note. The following abbreviations are used:
ND   Nuremberg Documents, from the *Trial of the Major War Criminals before the International Military Tribunal*; 42 volumes, Nuremberg, 1947–1949. (References are to documents presented in evidence.)
NP   Nuremberg Proceedings, from the *Trial of German Major War Criminals*; 22 parts, H.M.S.O., 1946–1950.

1   Adolf Hitler, *Mein Kampf* (Hurst and Blackett, Hutchinson Publishing Group 1939), p. 176
2   A. B. Keith, *Speeches and Documents on International Affairs* (Oxford University Press, 1938), Vol. I, p. 43
3   Keith, p. 50
4   Keith, p. 50
5   *The Times*, July 2nd, 1919, p. 11
6   *Mein Kampf*, p. 389
7   *Mein Kampf*, p. 387
8   *Mein Kampf*, p. 77
9   *Mein Kampf*, p. 78
10   *Mein Kampf*, p. 81
11   *Mein Kampf*, p. 79
12   *Mein Kampf*, p. 88
13   *Der Hitler Prozess* (Deutscher Volksverlag, München, 1924), p. 269
14   Kurt G. W. Ludecke, *I Knew Hitler* (Scribner's, New York, 1937), p. 82
15   *Der Hitler Prozess*, p. 150
16   *National Socialism* (U.S. State Department Publication 1864, Government Printing Office, Washington D.C., 1943), pp. 222–25
17   *Mein Kampf*, p. 24
18   Adolf Hitler, *Speech delivered in the Reichstag, January 30th, 1939* (Muller, Berlin), p. 14
19   *Mein Kampf*, p. 248
20   *Mein Kampf*, pp. 249–50
21   *Mein Kampf*, p. 467
22   *Mein Kampf*, p. 17
23   *Mein Kampf*, p. 126
24   *Mein Kampf*, p. 62
25   *Mein Kampf*, p. 65

26 *Speech Delivered in the Reichstag*, p. 42
27 Norman H. Baynes, ed., *The Speeches of Adolf Hitler* (Oxford University Press, 1942), Vol. I, p. 667
28 *Mein Kampf*, p. 48
29 *Mein Kampf*, p. 127
30 N.D. 789—PS
31 *Mein Kampf*, p. 100
32 *Mein Kampf*, p. 253
33 C. M. Bowra, *Memories 1898–1939* (Weidenfeld and Nicolson, 1966), p. 300
34 *Mein Kampf*, pp. 25–26
35 S. H. Roberts, *The House that Hitler Built*, (Methuen, 1938 ed.), p. 10
36 *Mein Kampf*, p. 330
37 *National Socialism*, pp. 34–37
38 *Speech Delivered in the Reichstag*, p. 17
39 *Mein Kampf*, p. 110
40 *Mein Kampf*, p. 159
41 *Mein Kampf*, p. 161
42 N.P. Part XXII, pp. 406–7
43 Hansard, *Parliamentary Debates*, 292 H.C. Deb. 5s. 13/7/34, p. 734
44 Roberts, pp. 138–9
45 William L. Shirer, *My Berlin Diary* (Hamish Hamilton, 1941), p. 26
46 Otto Strasser, *Hitler and I* (Cape, 1940), pp. 74–7
47 Shirer, pp. 118–19
48 Heinz Guderian, *Panzer Leader* (Michael Joseph, 1952), pp. 414–15
49 Roberts, p. 12
50 Sir Nevile Henderson, *Failure of a Mission* (Hodder and Stoughton, 1940), p. 177
51 Ludecke, p. 92
52 Roberts, p. 22
53 Strasser, p. 74
54 *Mein Kampf*, p. 554
55 N.D. 2949—PS
56 Godfrey Scheele, *The Weimar Republic* (Faber, 1946), p. 149
57 N.D. D—203
58 *The Times*, March 1st, 1933
59 *The Times*, March 1st, 1933
60 *The Times*, March 1st, 1933
61 *The Times*, March 24th, 1933
62 *The Times*, March 24th, 1933
63 *The Times*, March 25th, 1933

64 Baynes, Vol. I, p. 861
65 N.D. 614—PS
66 N.D. 1388—A—PS
67 Baynes, Vol. I, p. 372
68 Baynes, Vol. I, p. 388
69 Baynes, Vol. I, p. 189
70 Baynes, Vol. I, p. 315
71 Baynes, Vol. I, pp. 313 and 309
72 *Speech at Nuremberg, The New York Times*, September 16th, 1935
73 *Speech Delivered in the Reichstag*, p. 44
74 *The New York Times*, January 3rd, 1942
75 Roberts, p. 208
76 *Mein Kampf*, p. 357
77 N.D. 1856—PS
78 N.D. R—142
79 Baynes, Vol. I, pp. 321–22
80 N.D. 2499—PS
81 C. W. Guillebaud, *The Economic Recovery of Germany from 1933 to The Incorporation of Austria in March 1938* (Macmillan, 1939), p. 277
82 Guillebaud, pp. 212, 101, 218
83 Roberts, p. 265
84 Bowra, p. 278
85 N.D. 1918—PS
86 Hermann Rauschning, *Hitler Speaks* (Thornton Butterworth, 1939), p. 123
87 Roberts, p. 363
88 *Speech Delivered in the Reichstag*, p. 51
89 Keith, pp. 283–4
90 *The Times*, March 13th, 1936 (quoted Baynes, Vol. II, pp. 1302–3)
91 Baynes, Vol. I, p. 742
92 Baynes, Vol. II, pp. 1014–15
93 Baynes, Vol. II, p. 1432
94 Baynes, Vol. II, pp. 1585–86
95 *Documents concerning German–Polish Relations and the Outbreak of Hostilities between Great Britain and Germany on September 3rd, 1939*, Cmd, 6106 (H.M.S.O., 1939), p. 14
96 *Documents concerning German–Polish Relations*, p. 14
97 *Documents concerning German–Polish Relations*, p. 15
98 *Speech Delivered in the Reichstag*, p. 51
99 *Documents concerning German-Polish Relations*, p. 161
100 *Nazi-Soviet Relations 1939–1941* (U.S. State Department Publication 3023, Government Printing Office, Washington D.C., 1948), pp. 76–7
101 *Documents concerning German–Polish Relations*, p. 195

INCREASING PRESSURE.

David Low's view (*London Evening Standard* 17th February, 1938) of the Nazi pressure being applied to the Austrian Chancellor, Schuschnigg, and the in-